# SOCIAL MEDIA
## SECRETS FOR SALES

### POWERFUL PRACTICES FOR INCREASING SALES

SIMPLE SOCIAL MEDIA STRATEGIES FOR SALESPEOPLE
DRIVING TRAFFIC TO YOUR DOOR!

**Bernard Smalls**

# TABLE OF CONTENTS

⬤⬤⬤⬤⬤*re we share, the more we have..."*

# *Nearly Two-Thirds of Americans Use Social Media!*

## PREFACE

This knowledge has the potential power to change your sales career and your entire life!

The world in general has grossly underestimated the power of social media. It's time people, especially 'salespeople' to awake to the power of social media. Some people in business still have a negative attitude regarding social media. They still say; social media can't sell products and services! People do!

Don't commit financial suicide by cutting off the power of digital selling. Hey! There is a new sheriff in town! His name is Social Media! Awake to the new reality today and sell more of your product or service than you can imagine. **Let's go!**

# INTRODUCTION

*"SOCIAL MEDIA is not always an online distraction or procrastination platform. While some may be addicted to their social media networks, it is one of the best ways to stay informed."*

## - FORBES

We love social media for many reasons, but chief among them has to be the ability to engage directly with our friends and family. Social media is a powerful tool for keeping in contact with others. In retail sales of products and services social media can be used as a platform for nearly effortlessly talking directly to both your customers and your potential customers. In this regard social media is unmatched as a 'free' tool for marketing. Social media, when used properly helps your customer along the Path To A Sale. Welcome to Social Media Secrets for Sales!

The journey begins,

Bernard

# Social media is a powerful tool for keeping in contact with others.

# CHAPTER 1

## SOCIAL MEDIA: THE PATH TO A SALE

As a salesperson your success depends on your ability to get connect with and influence people. Connectivity is the major key to sales success. You would agree with that, wouldn't you? This is why you need to learn the social media secrets and start strategically using social media as a part of your sales strategy. Even for the established sales professional it's important that you at least open your mind to the use social media. In the digital-information age, this is just the new reality. Speed to the market is crucial today. Wouldn't you agree? No matter what your product or service, Social Media is a business generator because it is often the beginning point on the path to a sale. Remember it is a free tool for marketing, product exposure and customer relations.

## SOCIAL MEDIA: TODAY'S WOM

When I started selling, many of my sales were the result of referrals through WOM (word of mouth). We used the phone as the primary way of contact, with direct mail, aka snail-mail as the written way to follow up to get customers. With the instant nature of communication on social media, it is today's WOM. Why not use it to move potential buyers along on the path to the sale? In this book I will show you how.

The reality is that customer contact is made easier and faster through social media. Today you need an online network just like you needed your customer list of names and phone numbers back in the good old days.

# CHAPTER 2

# SPEED KILLS!

You have heard the phrase SPEED KILLS. We use that term often in business. We mean the faster you move the more sales and money you make. SPEED KILLS! Using Social Media will increase your greatest asset; Time. Social media is fast!!!

Simply said, because of how instantly you can create content, videos, etc. and communicate by social media, you simply save time. Does that make sense to you? Whether you are selling, homes, boats or automobiles Social media is a real game-changer. Recently, I was sitting in my car about to leave the house to go to Starbucks. I had an idea that I wanted to share with my 5,000 Facebook friends. I pulled out my iPhone, made a short Facebook Live video and posted it to my Facebook page in less than 15 minutes. The video quickly had over 200 viewers from Atlanta to Alaska! WOW!!! SPEED KILLS!

As an author, I sell books. I have found that in this digital age speed to the market is the key to selling lots of books. The same is true with any product or service. The first to get the 'eyes' of the customer and engage them often makes the sale. Because of the fierce competition in the digital market place SPEED KILLS! Your competition will do nearly anything to sell his product and the first to get the eyes of the prospect often gets the sale. Back in the day, we use to go to the mall and put out flyers. Today's flyer is social media. This has virtually put many out of the (paper) printing business. Many even use digital business cards instead of paper.

Today, you can go into your furniture showroom with a friend. Have her hold your cell phone and create a short video of your product, maybe you kicking back in an easy chair and post it for thousands of potential customer eyes in less than one-half hour. What part of that do you not want?

Again, SPEED KILLS! Some of the best sales managers I have ever known have continually used that phrase.

Now we all know that for most salespeople there's way too much time killed or downtime during the day. Why not put time to better use by using social media?

# A QUICK STRATEGY FOR KILLING IT!

Here's a quick social media strategy to jumpstart you, assuming that you are on Facebook.

1. You create content and share with 200 contacts.
2. Those 200 have the potential of influencing 200 contacts = 40,000 prospects.
3. Exposing your product to a potential 40,000 is way better than waiting for someone to walk in. Isn't it?

Even if you are not on Facebook, you can join now for FREE! You can easily build your Facebook up to 200 contacts, can't you? Your 200 contacts have 200 contacts so that means you have the potential of reaching 40,000 prospects on Facebook. Let's see; 40,000 people that may your product or service!! With the potential 40,000 customers reached, do you think any of them need or knows someone who needs what you sell? Come on man!!!

It's time to get started KILLING IT with Social Media.

# CHAPTER 3

## BUT, COMPUTERS CAN'T SELL PRODUCT!!

Some veteran salespeople and older sales managers say; "social media, yeah, that is easy for the millennial, but not necessary for sales veterans." Trust me, I have heard it. I have always been an early adopter. I got my first Mac laptop back in the mid 90s, the AOL days. My old General Manager in the automotive business use to often say, Bernard, you can play around on that computer all you want, "computers can't sell no cars!!!" Well, he eventually ended up getting fired from a dealership after 15 years on the job for not changing with the times. The business had simply passed him by. He did not value the Internet at first because he thought it was a lazy person's tool. However, after getting fired, he awoke to the power of digital marketing and ran another very successful dealership.

For one reason or another, many older people struggle with social media. Maybe it's because they feel like there's really only so much you can do or say online to get people to buy. Maybe it's because they think that social media is just a FAD.

Could be because they don't feel like they need to learn anything new.

I have found that many older car guys have a psychological block in regards to social media. This could be because their kids and grandkids spend so much time on it. The truth is you can sell more by using the influence of Social Media on the path to a sale!

## RELATIONSHIP SELLING

Let's face it. No matter what age you live in, you need constant contact with guests and referrals through word-of-mouth to be successful. Relationship selling is the most profitable way to build your sales business, no matter what you are selling. You sell to people! Social media is a major, major tool for online relationships.

If you follow these simple step-by-step strategies in this book, you'll build your network in no time at all. Soon you'll be engaging and attracting potential customers and selling your products. Getting started may seem overwhelming so I have created this program and step-by-step strategy to make using social media simple. *Let's go!!!*

WHY IS SOCIAL MEDIA SO IMPORTANT TO SALES SUCCESS TODAY?

_____

_____

WHAT HAS BEEN THE PREVAILING ATTITUDE ABOUT THE USE OF SOCIAL MEDIA IN GENERAL?

_____

_____ WHY

MUST WE CHANGE THIS ATTITUDE?

_____

_____

# CHAPTER 4

## SOCIAL MEDIA SECRETS FOR SALES

"Billions of people worldwide use social media networks. In terms of marketing, it is the most cost effective way to reach mass amounts of consumers." **- FORBES**

So, I'm sure that by now you have seen that social media is a tool to be used on the path to increased sales.

So the next question is, what are the best ones (forms of social media) to use for general sales? Good question!

Based on practical experience in building high performing sales teams, and being on the sales floor analyzing and giving feedback to managers and business owners in a variety of industries (I have sold everything from advertising to life insurance to my wife jewelry☺), I recommend a list of the best five (5) forms of social media to use in retail sales. This is based on the nature of retail sales and the psychology of selling. I have been in the sales business for a longtime, and I understand the nature of the beast.

Again, there may be others, but the following list of social media channels is best **in my years of experience** because they are most user-friendly for the nature of energy and relationship in sales.

**BERNARD"S TOP 5 SOCIAL MEDIA CHANNELS FOR SALES:**

1. FACEBOOK
2. TWITTER
3. INSTAGRAM
4. YOUTUBE
5. LINKEDIN

In this training program we will show you a few simple best practices for using the five channels of social media that are best suited for general sales of products and services.

# FACEBOOK

*...re we share, the more we have..."*

# CHAPTER 5

# HOW TO USE FACEBOOK IN SALES

**Facebook has nearly 2 billion users as of this writing.** Facebook is a powerful, powerful relationship building, contact communications tool. Why do you think it has grown so large and so fast? One psychological reason is that people are social beings and they have a need to share with others. Even, down to a picture of the hamburger that they are about to consume ☺.

As a social networking tool, Facebook provides benefits for business and individuals too, such as making a group, chatting with clients, making an event, wall stickers, reliable platforms, news feed, video, Facebook Live and more. You can meet new people and even gain **knowledge** about various places, traditions and cultures.

Why is Facebook so important for you sales success? It's simple. Facebook allows any user to record live videos and share them with friends. How valuable is that in sales? In sales, exposure is king!!! Individuals can use this to their advantage in several ways to market products and services and provide a behind-the-scenes experience to customers.

Here are three powerful reasons to use Facebook in car sales:

1. **Facebook has nearly 2 billion users!!!**
2. **Facebook is free!**
3. **Google and Facebook work together!**

We all know that Google owns the Internet. Google is so popular that the name has become a verb. Just Google it! ☺ There are major benefits for using Facebook in sales.

## FACEBOOK AS A PRIMARY CHANNEL

Out of all social media, Facebook is the undisputed champion of the world. Because of this I suggest that you make it your primary channel. Why should a retail salesperson select Facebook as the primary digital marketing channel? *Entrepreneur* Magazine says that Facebook is the number one marketing channel of all social media.

### *What are the major benefits of Facebook in sales?*

Marketing is the key to success for any business. If you're already a salesperson or planning to launch your career in car sales, it's crucial to have your digital marketing strategy in place right away. THIS IS THE FAST TRACK TO SALES SUCCESS. I have seen numerous sales people with no experience lead the sales board within 60 days by using a social media marketing strategy. Understanding the basics of digital marketing is a critical success factor in sales in today's markets.

**Facebook beats all other digital marketing channels for the individual salesperson.**

**MAJOR BENEFITS!**

What are the major benefits of Facebook in sales?

Here are the 7 reasons why it makes the most sense for a salesperson to use Facebook.

### 1. Friendship targeted audience

Facebook is built around friendship. That is why they call your followers on Facebook FRIENDS – duh ☺. Selling to people who like and know you is the best way to get started in sales. For this reason, I train new salespeople to contact people that they know FIRST. Creating a WHO DO YOU KNOW list to prospect for sales works... Facebook is basically a great way to let people know about your new sales profession.

### 2. Maximum visibility at minimum cost

If you're in sales, you want to go where the people are. Facebook has approximately 2 billion active monthly users and is a FREE channel (Unless you choose to buy ads). Also, Facebook Live is free.

Research shows that consumers spend 90% of time on mobile is on apps and Facebook leads the way as the most downloaded free platform. You can also buy Facebook ads. These numbers are simply too big to ignore.

*re we share, the more we have..."*

## 3. Brand awareness! You are the brand!

Facebook can work a lot like PR if managed strategically.

Brand Awareness for you in sales means getting the attention of people and letting them know what you do and what your product is. The attention grabbing power of Facebook provides maximum exposure for you quickly. Getting started with Facebook as a new salesperson you can instantly have a bigger audience. The goal is simple. Capture attention to get in front of people most likely to be interested in your product or service.

## 4. Facebook Live

Today, video is the heavyweight champion of customer engagement. Facebook Live was recently introduced to users and has taken the Internet by storm. It allows any user to record live videos and share them with friends.

*Salespeople can use this to their advantage in several ways.*

> ➤ Provide a behind-the-scenes experience to customers.
> ➤ Show sneak previews of new products or updates.
> ➤ Promote events.
> ➤ Answer questions.

People spend 3xs longer watching live video than reading native content. With this in mind, it's becoming a requirement to include videos in Facebook marketing.

## 5. Quick feedback

In the old days, when businesses wanted to reach out their customer base for feedback on products or services, they would have to do things like direct-mail, voting polls or cold call surveys. Those days are over and brands need to look no further than social media.

Facebook makes it easy for individuals and businesses to simply post a question on their status and sit back and watch for the comments.

Time is perhaps the most valuable asset in business. Facebook is great for salespeople looking to make an impression of their image and product quickly by posting content, videos etc., so they can see what works and what doesn't quickly, without hassle.

## 6. Power of W.O.M.

W.O.M. is an acronym for word-of-mouth, the most trusted form of advertising! One of the biggest advantages of Facebook (or social media in general) is that it gives everyone a voice that will be heard. In addition to providing the ability to share opinions on products or services, Facebook enables users to endorse businesses within their own community by simply hitting the "Like" button. As you create raving fan customers who buy from you and post pictures of happy customers on Facebook, the power of WOM (word of mouth) is exponentially released.  9 in 10 consumers take the words of their peers into account during the buying process. Why not let your customers do the talking for you on Facebook? It's The Power of Good old W.O.M!!!

## 7. Growth

Facebook is improving and growing by the day. In the last four years the number of users has almost doubled. The future is looking very bright. There will be more users to show your products and services to and advertising will likely keep getting better and cheaper. This is a very exciting time for sales. Sales professionals should prepare to use Facebook a significant part of their marketing strategy. There is no denying that Facebook is here to stay. It's amazing to think that what started as a simple way to stay in touch with friends has turned into a platform that connects people and brands all across the world.

### Facebook BUSINESS pages Salespeople

To get more exposure in the use of Facebook, you can create you own brand by developing a business page. This is a great tool for the user who is prepared to invest in marketing. My advice is that after you have started using Facebook for friends, you should consider a business page.

### Top 8 Benefits of a Facebook Business Page

1. Increased Exposure to Potential Customers.
2. 2 BILLION USERS.
3. Gather More Leads.
4. Inexpensive.
5. Reach a Targeted Audience.
6. Use Facebook Insights.
7. Build Brand Loyalty.
8. Increase Your Traffic. (Without waiting for walk-ins)

## *GETTING STARTED WITH FACEBOOK*

### 1. Create Your Profile.

If you already have a Facebook profile then you're one step ahead. If not, simply sign up for Facebook and walk through the simple steps to create your profile. Keep in mind that you're now sales 'professional' on Facebook so act accordingly. You can share info about yourself but always keep in mind that you're presenting a brand called YOU.

### 2. Set Your Goals.

**Here are some questions to answer:**

- Who do you want to attract?
- What do you want to say them?
- Where do your customers live and work?
- When will you post content?
- How will you execute your goals?

**One of your goals could be to get 200 contacts in a week.** Use the "Find Friends" app on Facebook to look for people you know. Start asking your customers if they're on Facebook and put out a friend request to them. Make sure you mention they "like" the store's Facebook page too! Develop your social media consciousness!

### 3. Create Content.

Content is what you post on your Facebook wall to engage your customer. My motto is simple: "The more we share, the more we have..."

re we share, the more we have..."

You want your content to be three things:

*Relevant!*
*Recent!*
*Local!*

You can search thousands of blogs out there that deliver great information all the time and repost that which is relevant...

You can share video testimonials.

You can share your store's content.

By the way, don't oversell on Facebook. It's ok to post this week's ad but remember to share or "solve" 80% of the time and "sell" 20% of the time. This is the 80/20 Rule. Create content with value.

### 4. Execute Your Plan.

Make every attempt to post 8 -10 times per day. Yes, 8 -10 times a day!! This may seem exorbitant, **but social media is noisy, so you must be loud!!** This may sound like a lot of posting at first but once you get the rhythm going it will become second nature.

You want to post regularly because Facebook's algorithms (computer data procedures) are set to constantly facilitate engagement. If you DO NOT engage, your posts will not appear on others' walls and you won't maintain those relationships. ENGAGE! ENGAGE! ENGAGE!

## 5. **Analyze Your Results.**

It's essential to monitor your success. You want to see which content is getting the best reactions from your network. You can do this easily in the beginning by just reviewing daily what your results were. Once you get a larger Social network you'll need monitoring tools. But for now, YOU are the monitoring tool. JUST PAY ATTENTION to what people are responding too and keep count. For example; if you are in real-estate and you post a picture on an old house built in Charleston, South Carolina in the 1800s and you get a lot of engagement, post more older historic homes. Pay attention to the engagement patterns.

### What is tagging and how does it work?

Use tagging when it is appropriate. Why tagging? When you tag someone, you create a link to his or her profile. The post you tag the person in may also be added to that person's timeline (if they allow it). For example, you can tag a photo to show who's in the photo or post a status update and say who you're with. If you tag a friend in your status update, anyone who sees that update can click on your friend's name and go to their profile. Your status update may also show up on that friend's timeline (if they allow it).

To tag someone:
1. Open Facebook
2. Create a post
3. Type @ and the friends name
4. Tap and post!

The post will now show on your timeline and the individuals you tagged (again, if they allow it), giving exposure to all of your friends and their friends. That's POWER MARKETING! And it's free!!! Try practicing this now, before you get a real customer.

Finally, us the hash tag #ravingfans to gain even more exposure on Facebook. Try this now and tap the #ravingfans. Wow! Amazing stuff!

**LET'S GET IT STARTED!!!**

After you've put together your plan, jump in! Get started! Sales success is waiting for you now!

It's not enough to "dip your toe into the waters of social media" so dive in and make the commitment to yourself and your future customers. Social Media is not instant gratification. It takes time like all business relationships so be patient and don't forget to have fun!

**FACEBOOK BEST PRACTICES**

1. *USE THE 80/20 RULE (SHARE/SELL)*
2. *POST 8-10 TIMES A DAY!*
3. *ASK QUESTIONS ON POSTS…*
4. *TAG RAVING FANS*
5. *USE THE HASH TAG #ravingfans*

# THINKTANK

**THINK TANK**

1. WHAT IS THE MAJOR REASON FOR USING FACEBOOK TO INFLUENCE SALES?

_____

_____

_____

2. NAME 3 POOR PRACTICES IN USING FACEBOOK TO BUILD BUSINESS:

_____

_____

_____

3. HOW DOES THE 80/20 RULE APPLY IN USING FACEBOOK?

_____

_____

_____

# *TWITTER*

# CHAPTER 6

# HOW TO USE TWITTER

Now please understand; we are talking about increasing sales, not just selling products on the Internet or social media. The million-dollar question you must answer is; what's the consumer's path to a purchase? I admit, Twitter cannot sell your product but it is a signpost on the path to a sale. Twitter is one of the most neglected channels for influencing sales at the retail level. You are gaining secrets in this section that will give you a definite competitive advantage and make you a sales champion. You are learning How to be a Social Media Sales Champion!

**The Twitter Social Media Strategy:**

Of the social media platforms, Twitter may be one of the most difficult for sales people to embrace. This is obvious by the lack of use of this channel by retail salespeople. The character limit, the fleeting nature of the information, the careful balance between spamming your audience with tweets and tweeting frequently enough to even be remembered. It's a bit much for a lot of salespeople, until they understand the strategic plan for using Twitter.

My experience teaches that Twitter is not the place for selling, but for influencing the path to sales.

**Here are some effective, foolproof practices for Twitter.**

**1. Share the Dealership Culture**

One of the best things about businesses is that they almost all have a sense of workplace culture, and that's unique. People like to do business with companies that don't feel like a faceless money-hole. Use Twitter to post about company culture and pride. Now obviously, a businesses Twitter feed can't be entirely devoted to self-congratulating, but a little of "this is who we are," is an excellent choice.

**2. Happy Customers**

**Happy customers are social media currency** that not a lot of businesses are sure how to spend. If you are in car sales, posting a picture with a new beautiful car and the happy owner – and tagging that owner – is a great way to encourage referrals, spread the dealership's name, and show that we care for customers. Remember; "People don't care how much you know until they know how much you care."

### 3. Popular Culture:

Now we all realize that you can over emphasize your own greatness in any arena. YOU CAN BE A LEGEND IN YOUR OWN MIND! Most people are not the biggest fans of when organizations or salespeople over-extend themselves with their social media. We have all seen it. For example, don't bore people stiff with pictures of food. Staying within the realm of your product while still engaging with some of the most talked-about pop-culture events is usually effective. Tweets regarding pop culture show that you have connection to what's going on in the world – something shoppers like to see from businesses. We all love it!

### 4. Reputation Management

We love social media for many reasons, but chief among them has to be the ability to engage directly with our audience. One major area you can use Twitter in is customer experience and online reputation.

Use twitter to encourage happy customers to leave online reviews at sites like Yelp and Google Reviews. Communicate the guarantee of excellent customer service. On Google reviews, strive for 5 stars. Shoot for the moon! 4.6 is a number that would be impressive for any business.

*re we share, the more we have..."*

# TWITTER BEST PRACTICES

1. *POST 8-10 TIMES A DAY!*

2. *POST ABOUT THE CULTURE!*

3. *ASK FOR REVIEWS!*

4. *SHOOT FOR THE MOON!*

5. *MANAGE YOUR REPUTATION*

**THINK TANK**

1. WHY SHOULD YOU USE TWITTER TO BUILD YOUR BUSINESS?

_____

_____

2. IS TWITTER THE BEST PLACE TO POST PICTURES OF MERCHANDISE? (WHY/WHYNOT?)

_____

_____

3. HOW CAN YOU USE TWITTER AS A REPUTATION BUILDER?

_____

_____

# *INSTAGRAM*

*re we share, the more we have..."*

# CHAPTER 7

# HOW TO USE INSTAGRAM IN SALES

Instagram in sales? Why Instagram? What the heck is Instagram? Instagram is a mobile photo-and video-sharing social media platform that has been growing rapidly since it started in 2010. The popular social media app says it now has **800 million users**, Instagram also said it has 500 million daily active users. A new Pew Research Center survey finds that **35 percent** of U.S. adults use Instagram — an increase of **7 percent** from 2016.

## WHY INSTAGRAM?

Things are changing rapidly in the marketplace and in media. People are dumping cable and over-the-air TV in favor of online streaming such as Netflix, Hulu and Amazon Prime. As they do so, they are also flocking to a myriad of new social platforms like Snapchat, Pinterest and Instagram. Why shouldn't you do the same in your sales business? Why shouldn't you change with the times?

Besides from the growing audience, Instagram offers features that cannot be found on other platforms. Users are drawn to its simplicity and visually stunning content. And as a bonus, Instagram plays well with others. The app is seamlessly integrated with Facebook, Twitter, Tumblr and Flickr so you can share your post immediately or save and share later. This handy feature can be a big time saver.

With more than 800 million users sharing millions of photos and videos each day, it's hard to find a reason not to be on this fast growing social media network, especially since you are in sales. You do want to reach more people as a salesperson, don't you? If you are looking to expand your customer outreach in sales, Instagram is a social media tool to consider.

## SET UP AN INSTAGRAM ACCOUNT

### 1. SET-UP

First things first: download the app on your phone and create an account using your name or a close variation. For example, "bernardsmalls" is my Instagram name." Once you are signed up, you will have full reign to update your profile with a picture, name, website link and brief description. Try to keep it consistent with your retail business branding, but feel free to be creative. You can always edit the profile later with a different link or picture.

### 2. STRATEGY

What would you like to get out of Instagram? Perhaps you want to use the platform to find new customers, promote a specific product or service, share your company culture, or discover the latest industry trends. Whatever your aim, just make sure you have a clear strategy for using Instagram rather than simply using it to share any content with a photo.

*re we share, the more we have..."*

## 3. FOLLOWERS

Remember the struggle to get Facebook likes or Google+ followers when you first started? The great news is, starting a follower base is not as difficult on Instagram (I had 317 followers before I posted my first picture). As soon as you start your account, you have the option to follow other people based on your Facebook account, phone contacts, or by searching. If your brand is relevant to those you follow, then they will likely follow you back. Also, your Facebook contacts on Instagram will get a notification when you join, which will help drive followers. These features will help you initiate a following, but in order to keep followers and gain a wider audience you will need to start posting content.

## 4. POSTS

Do not hesitate to post content. Especially pictures of unusual or sporty vehicles. Fortunately, Instagram lets you use photos directly from your phone's native camera app. If you don't have a ton of content right off the back, reuse a few old photos to help build up your portfolio. Then add a quick message including a few key hash tags to describe the photo. You will quickly realize that hash tags are not optional on Instagram. They (#hashtags) are crucial to users being able to find and ultimately start following you. Also add tags if your photo includes a particular person, place, or brand.

Last but not least, remember that Instagram is a social network. Engage with your fans by liking and commenting on other posts and checks back to see if someone posed a question that needs answering. Instagram requires some extra attention, but it can be a worthwhile expansion for any kind of sales. The best way to find out if it works is to dive in and launch an account. Let's do it!

## PRACTICAL TIPS FOR SALES SUCCESS

### TIP 1: POST TO INSTAGRAM CONSISTENTLY

Using a mix of "organic" images from the store along with your images of products allows you to maintain a presence on the platform without spending tons of time thumbing at your phone on the retail sales floor. To share an existing non-phone image from your computer, we suggest using third-party sites like gramblr.com or latergram. me. Or, if you'd rather stick with your phone, email the photo to yourself, open it on your phone and then save the image to your photo library on your phone. This will allow you to open and post the image on Instagram on your phone.

### TIP 2: SHOW OFF FEATURES WITH INSTAGRAM VIDEOS

Don't be afraid to share details about your product, such as features and benefits. People don't buy features, they buy benefits. We often work so closely with our own products that we forget how awesome they are, and there is no better way to share those awesome benefits than with Instagram.

*re we share, the more we have..."*

## TIP 3: KEEP IT REAL

Yes – It's important to make sure people are aware of your store and your products and your sales, but you don't have to shout all the time. **Do some listening**, and you'll learn about your target audience and their needs. Instagram is, after all, a social medium. One way to keep it real is to post things that *aren't* products for sale. (GASP! I know – right?) Real people buy products from real people. Your Instagram feed should reflect that you are a REAL person, not just a salesperson.

Share photos that express your real time thoughts and comments. We've learned in the past that photos including people (customers, employees, etc.) yield much higher engagement rates than photos of inanimate objects, such as motorcycles, suits, or cars on a lot. Post photos of people, do your share of liking posts from other people, make some comments, spark a conversation and enjoy.

## TIP 4: GEOLOCATION ON INSTAGRAM

One of the most powerful ways to boost likes and comments on Instagram is to tag a location in your post as you post it. According to the previously mentioned study by Simply Measured, Instagram posts with locations get a whopping 79% more engagement.

Before you publish your post, search for and pick the most relevant spot on the map. Your image is then "geotagged" onto the map, and if anyone peruses your local area on the map, they'll stumble upon your photo or video.

**TIP 5: ASK A QUESTION. GET ANSWERS!**

If you want comments on your Instagram posts (who doesn't?), just ASK for them! For example:

An image of a convertible with the top down on a sunny day might get a decent amount of likes, but only one or two comments. To really get the ball rolling, you could ask: "Who would you want to ride shotgun with me in this convertible?"

Another way to drive engagement is to have people vote on a simple "election." For example, post the image of an old 'brick' cellular phone model next to a new one and asked their followers to chime in.

**CONNECTING WITH PEOPLE**

Unlike more seasoned social networks, Instagram has less "fluff" making the platform simple for users. Focus your efforts on key business categories that win on Instagram.

**4 Key Areas**

**1. EVENTS**

There is no event too small for Instagram (such as a company potluck). It is a great way to document an event and easily capture photos. Use your account to show behind the scenes action, ask for feedback or communicate a particular session at your event.

## 2. PRODUCTS

Think of your posts as a way to show and tell your followers about your products. Through photos and videos, you have the opportunity to teach people about what you sell. Whether that is finding the right home for a growing family or a pre-owned vehicle for a college student. This helps bring life and ownership to products, ultimately setting them apart from the competition.

## 3. SALES

If you are running specials or giveaways, definitely cross post them on Instagram. Also consider running an Instagram-only promotion. It can help boost allegiance from those that already follow you as well as helping gain new loyal followers.

## 4. CULTURE

Showing off your company culture is the easiest and most fun way to humanize your Instagram. A picture of the warehouse manager cutting his birthday cake with accounting staff cheering him on speaks volumes about your culture. Doing this is detouring away from what you sell and showing off the team and the culture instead.

## MEASURING INSTAGRAM SUCCESS

Without setting appropriate goals or benchmarks, your social media marketing, like anything else becomes the Wild, Wild West. You need to have goals before you can measure success. For Instagram specifically, set goals for likes, comments and new followers. Think in terms of how many followers you have and what percentage you expect to interact with each post.

One model suggests that for every 1000 followers there should be a total 37 likes and comments. Keep track of your benchmarks and update them at least monthly if not weekly.

## TIME OF DAY

Typically Instagram is most popular in the late afternoon and into the evening. Posting between 5pm and 8pm is a safe bet, but do not be afraid to stray. Look at past Instagram posts and compare how they performed on certain days and times. (Tip: a good reporting app is a great tool for this).

In addition to the perfect time of day, post consistently rather than binge 'gramming.' Instagram posts typically have a longer shelf life than other social media channels so space out your posts even if you have a dozen awesome photos to share in one day.

## THE BEST CONTENT WINS

Take the plunge and post some video content. Did your followers feverishly engage with the video? Then post more videos! You can post the most beautiful content everyday but it may not be the right material for your customers. Diversify your posts and see what ends up receiving the most engagement so you can find the best path for sales through your Instagram account. Your followers will thank you!

## INSTAGRAM BEST PRACTICES

1. *ADD PICTURES OF 4 TO 5 PRODUCTS DAILY*

2. *CONNECT WITH PEOPLE*

3. *USE GOOD CREDIT, BAD CREDIT, NO CREDIT (if apropos)*

4. *REMEM- CLOSED MOUTHS DON'T GET FED*

5. *THE BEST CONTENT WINS*

## THINK TANK

1. WHAT PERCENTAGE OF ADULTS USE INSTAGRAM?

_____

_____

2. HOW IS THIS PLATFORM BEST UTILIZED IN SALES?

_____

_____

3. WHY IS IT IMPORTANT TO USE (#) HASHTAGS WITH INSTAGRAM PICTURES?

_____

_____

# *YOUTUBE*

*re we share, the more we have..."*

# CHAPTER 8

# HOW TO USE YOUTUBE

***One thing I know for sure, that is you can Sell More Cars Using YouTube Videos.***

Use of videos for promoting products and services has become extremely common nowadays. So, it's obvious that any high profile industry would also jump on the bandwagon. There's no way one can deny the immense impact a video can have on the target market but if you want to increase your sales, you must make sure that the videos created by you are powerful enough to attract your target customers. Read through this section to get acquainted with the benefits of using YouTube videos for selling products and learn different ways of attracting more people towards the products offered by you.

## Benefits of Using YouTube Videos for Selling

As a salesperson your goal should always be to discover new and effective ways of making people aware of what you have to sell, but without spending too much money. Advertising and promoting through YouTube Videos is probably the most cost-effective way of reaching a huge customer base in a high-impact way.

## BENEFITS OF THIS INFORMATION

**You will be able to take advantage of the huge reach of YouTube.** The reach of YouTube videos is increasing exponentially with every passing day. Today, it is the third most frequently visited website (after Google and social networking site Facebook) in the world and the second largest search engine (after Google).

Recently obtained numbers suggest that more than 1 billion people visit YouTube each month. Videos uploaded on this platform have the potential of reaching more US residents aged between 18 and 34 than all the cable networks operating currently. So, if you upload videos that are entertaining and informative, you will be able to reach a massive number of raving fan customers.

**Marketing via YouTube videos will make you more visible on Google.** As a retail salesperson the use of YouTube videos will definitely help you achieve your sales goal because Google owns YouTube. GOOGLE OWNS THE INTERNET!!! The Google Universal Search allows images, news, local searches, books, and of course videos to be blended together on Google's search results. Right now, Google considers videos as essential as the text-only web pages.

**You will see your audience promoting you.** If you succeed in making interesting videos showcasing the products and services you offer, conversions will take place more frequently and easily. If you are a hair-stylist, people would rather deal with someone they know and trust than to have to build trust. Videos create relationships. I often meet people who feel like they know me because of watching my videos, even though we have never met.

Whatever you sell, you will have to relate to your target audience effectively. Once you succeed in this, you can get people to view your videos promoting your offerings via comments and likes.

*re we share, the more we have..."*

You can use your YouTube channel for bringing targeted traffic 24 hours a day, no matter what your business. The best thing about these channels is that they not only drive good traffic but they do that without taking a single penny from you. Treat the YouTube channel as the hub for all the video content you create. Yes, creating the right kind of videos is extremely important for attracting visitors, but optimizing your YouTube channel is equally important, if not more.

## TYPES OF YOUTUBE VIDEO YOU MUST MAKE TO SELL MORE

This knowledge has the potential power to change your sales career and your entire life! If you can make your videos with a friend and yourself, you would actually be able to use this tool without spending a single penny. There are virtually no marketing tools that can work as effectively as YouTube videos. However, to enjoy the benefits of these videos, you must know what kind of videos will work for you. The discussion below will help you understand the types of video you must make to sell more products.

### 1. Testimonial videos-

These videos can be your best bet if you want to generate a feeling of authenticity among your existing customers. You must be wondering how they are different from written testimonials. Well, the written testimonials simply don't have the power of the testimonial videos. As it is tough to fake the videos, they appear more credible to people. Due to this reason, they have the ability to touch the hearts of more and more prospective buyers.

We are not trying to say that people who use written testimonials to promote their product are doing things in an absolutely wrong way. What we are trying to say here is that the effects of videos are more profound.

People tend to get attracted to uncommon things more easily than things they come across regularly. This makes the suggestion of creating testimonial videos a valid one.

We would suggest you to make videos featuring genuine customers. Modern-day consumers are extremely intelligent. If you try to fake them, they will not take a second to understand your objective. Record a minimum of 5 testimonials and use the best ones from continually.

A common mistake salespeople make when creating testimonial videos is not adding a suitable and convincing CTA (call to action). Don't forget to add one to your video if you want to convert YouTube traffic into sales. The CTA you use must be creative and unique. If you don't add a CTA, your viewers will have no clue what they should do next.

## 2. Videos with product reviews-

Product review videos are not as uncommon as the testimonial videos. As these videos are not rare, you must make sure that the ones you are making and uploading boast features that will allow them to stand out in the crowd. In other words, you must make the videos count. Don't be afraid to innovate!

*re we share, the more we have..."*

## 3. Put in immense effort to plan your videos out.

Instead of talking about all the basic features of the product you are trying to sell, cover 2 to 3 prominent features of that product in a single video. If you want to cover the other features, make more videos. You can use CTA to direct viewers of the first video to the others. Video titles should be enough for the viewers to understand what they should expect from the videos.

**The product review videos you will be uploading on your YouTube channel should be short and snappy.**

They should provide visitors with useful and essential information and should contain only the facts the title promises them to offer. Right at the end of the videos, add CTAs like "Dial 888-888-8888 to get in touch with me." Remember to give your name with a name hook. Example: Ask for Bernard, like St. Bernard ☺

## 4. Comparison videos-

Comparison videos can do wonders for you. COMPARE YOUR PRODUCT with their fiercest rivals and explain what makes your offerings the best. Focus just on 3 to 4 key factors that make the product you offer the best option for your potential customers.

## 5. FAQ videos-

The videos should make viewers feel relieved as they can see you are trying to solve their problems. **They should never feel that you have created the videos with the aim of impressing people so that**

**they purchase your product from you.** Upload as many FAQ videos as possible on your YouTube Channel. BASED ON the phone calls and emails you receive on daily basis, you know that customers come up with new questions almost every other day. While, FAQs are primarily about questions that are asked frequently, you shouldn't ignore questions that are although not asked very often, are extremely relevant. **One video shouldn't answer more than one question.** This is important as your potential customers must come across your video on the search engine results after typing a question only if the key phrase (the question) entered by him/her is similar to that of the title of your video. CTAs such as "Call us at 888-888-8888 to know more" are great companions of these videos.

**6. Videos with tips and valuable info-**

Examples of such videos include videos elaborating principles you live by when doing business, with maintenance tips to keep product in good shape. If you are selling cars, use tips for choosing a car for a large family or a small family and so on. In short, these videos should inform your target audience about your knowledge of your product. End them with catchy CTAs such as "Take a look at our website for more info on our products."

## Conclusion

I know that you are probably not an expert in making videos. However, as a sales consultant you have immense knowledge about the products you are offering. So, instead of trying to be too fancy, just concentrate on what you know and follow the guidelines that I have provided in this book. You would surely find your YouTube videos helping you in selling more products and services.

*"The more we share, the more we have..."*

# THINK TANK

## THINK TANK

**1.** WHY IS YOUTUBE SO IMPORTANT IN THE SOCIAL MEDIA MARKETING MIX?

_____

_____

_____

**2.** WHO OWNS YOUTUBE?

_____

_____

**3.** WHY SHOULD YOU NOT 'OVERSELL' ON YOUTUBE?

_____

_____

# *LINKEDIN*

# CHAPTER 9

# HOW TO USE LINKEDIN

LinkedIn is your online professional profile.

LinkedIn is the best 'business profile' social media for salespeople. LinkedIn is rapidly becoming the Facebook of the white-collar worker and you can benefit IF you use it to your advantage. When LinkedIn first began it was comparable to a large corporate conference that was not serving alcohol; most people just stuck to themselves in the corner and handed out business cards under the table. The Consultants saw this opportunity and used it as a platform to share how "awesome" they were. LinkedIn fought back with groups, Celebrity Influencers, and Pulse to try and keep the content streamlined towards business.

## STRICTLY BUSINESS

The content makeup of LinkedIn, though not 100% business isn't a bad thing; at least there are no baby photos yet! Even though the content is changing, the legitimacy of LinkedIn remains. This means, the more people use it as their dominant social stream, the more you can do as a salesperson to turn it into your personal CRM (customer relationship management) tool.

Now, let me show you some best practices for LinkedIn:

First, if you don't have a LinkedIn profile, wake up!

Whatever hang-ups you have about being social online are irrelevant. **During the most recently reported quarter, LinkedIn had 467 million members, up from 450 million members in the preceding quarter.** Every second, two new members are added, putting you further behind the curve. Unless you're engaged with it, sooner or later you will lose out for not participating if you haven't already.

Secondly, See LinkedIn as your online professional profile.

Understand and remember that trust is an essential component of the sales equation; customers are very hesitant to open their wallet when there is a feeling of uncertainty. Building trust also takes time – time you could be spending on building value in the product and your brand. Like with a referral, the ideal situation is to have a trustworthy persona established before you even meet a customer for the first time.

Finally, one challenge on your way to being trustworthy is to manage your reputation online. This isn't just for businesses, but salespeople as well. Whenever I meet a new person the first thing I do is search for them online. Your customers are doing the same, whether you know it or not. Having zero presence on LinkedIn is certainly not a positive thing; it puts you in the "faceless" category where all the "bad salespeople" exist.

LinkedIn not only allows you to showcase your professional achievements, but it also acts as a perceived independent third-party advisory to your character. If you are open and honest online, it lends to the belief you are the same in real life, say in a negotiation situation, for example. Even without recommendations, endorsements or shared connections (more on that later), having a profile shows a customer you are accessible, accountable, and most importantly, trustworthy. It shows that you did not just get out of jail last week.

Once you have a profile up and running, during your sales process it should become habitual that you ask if you can connect with your customers on LinkedIn. Remember, over 400 million people have LinkedIn.

A best practice is to have the customer add your profile, so when you leave them alone to check availability of your product or to get information about a service, the first thing they do is stalk your profile and hopefully add you. By the way, if they are busy looking you up, they won't be price-shopping your competitors. :)

When done properly, it begins to build trust from a third-party source, fortifying the impression you have given off during the rapport building process. If they don't add you right away, you should remind the customer before the customer leaves. You may be surprised that a customer may be more willing to add you on LinkedIn than to give out their email address. The average person is more vain than you think; everyone wants to hit that 500+ followers mark.

The more customers you have in your wheelhouse, the more beneficial the other aspects of the LinkedIn tool will be.

## BEST PRACTICES FOR LINKED IN

1. *BECOME A RESOURCE THAT PEOPLE WANT TO SHARE…*
2. *BUILD YOUR BUSINESS PROFILE*
3. *PROJECT THAT YOU ARE A PROFESSIONAL*
4. *BUILD THIRD PARTY CREDIBILITY*

## THINK TANK

1. WHAT IS THE MAIN PURPOSE OF LINKEDIN?

_____

_____

2. WHAT'S A WRONG USE OF THIS PLATFORM?

_____

_____

3. HOW CAN YOU USE LINKEDIN TO INFLUENCE MORE SALES?

_____

_____

# CHAPTER 10

## INCREASING YOUR SOCIAL MEDIA ENGAGEMENT

I have lived what I am telling you in this book! I personally have thousands of followers on a variety of social media and have sold lots of self-help/inspirational products and training books. As of today my MTD (month to date) listeners on my Positive Thinking Internet radio is well tracking well over 100,000 listeners. When I started 3 years ago I had one (1) listener – me! Since I am a corporate trainer in the automotive field, many of them (my followers) are in car sales. I've noticed that the types of posts they share fall into a very predictable pattern:

- Buy a car from me!
- Here is a great car for sale!
- I just sold a car and here is a pic/video of my customer!
- Here is something personal!

They repeat the cycle over and over again and it becomes so predictable that it's too easy for followers to tune these posts out.
Einstein said; "Insanity is doing the same thing over and over expecting a different result!"

When I teach the topic of social media marketing in my dealership training sessions or sales seminars, I often hear these things, "But I don't know what else I can share" or "I'd like to start doing videos but I'm not sure what I could talk about."

*re we share, the more we have..."*

**I want to give you some powerful ideas for social media posts that will have these benefits for you:**

- Break the repetitive cycle that everyone else is doing
- Make your posts more relevant and interesting
- Invite your followers to engage with you and go to you for their next purchase

I want you to consider adding variety to what you share to make your posts more relevant and interesting to your audience. Here are some additional ideas for your social media posts. For each one, there are many applications! Each category can be a video or a written post and is suited for most social media platforms: Facebook, YouTube, Twitter, Instagram, LinkedIn, etc.

**10 Ideas to Increase Social Media Engagement**

**1. A "How to" Message**

This category is the most underutilized and the most critical to raising your higher authority-based influencing. If you do this, it will help your customers see you as the expert.

**2. Product Tutorials**

This is not the same as a product presentation. Choose 1 feature or 1 helpful piece of info that your customer will find useful and do a post on it. Examples: How to set up Alexa in your home. How to program your Bluetooth; or how to program the new garage door opener. The idea is to provide an answer to a common question.

### 3. What you love about your job

People like doing business with people who love what they do! Your job doesn't have to be perfect for you to like something about it. What is your favorite part of selling your product? What do you like about the sales? What do you like about the brand you sell? Do a video highlighting your personal likes or share your thoughts in a post or blog.

### 4. "What to Expect" Post

Do you assume that your future customers understand what will happen if they come to buy from you today? Create posts where you share what they'll expect from you and your store. Highlight essential parts of the process as well as unique things you'll do as part of your personal brand.

### 5. Product Demonstration

This category may be more conducive to a video format. For some of the ideas, you may also need to do some advance planning or get help from a colleague. Don't limit yourself to a video of yourself! Take your best-selling product and cover a few key benefits.

### 6. Facility Tour

This can be done by doing a video facility tour or writing a social media post about it. Describe your stores unique competitive advantages, share your awards, or do an overview of customer amenities.

## 7. Interview with Management

Why do customers have to meet your manager only when something has gone wrong? Like when you are not happy with your food at a restaurant. Create posts where you interview your management. Ideas for interview topics: why they hired you, their satisfaction guarantee, the history of the business, or their mission statement.

## 8. Your thoughts about the business overall

Educate your audience about the industry you are in and about buying trends. You can create your own posts or share informative articles written by industry experts. Share what is happening nationally, what is happening with your brand, or what is happening with your local market. I recommend that you do 2 ideas per week. Add more variety, interest and wider application to your posts and you will see more engagement and eventually more business!

# THINKTANK

**THINK TANK**

1. WHAT ARE THREE OF THE MAIN BENEFITS IN USING SOCIAL MEDIA?

   _____

   _____

   _____

2. WHAT ARE THREE WRONG WAYS TO USE SOCIAL MEDIA?

   _____

   _____

   _____

# CHAPTER 11

# WELCOME TO THE PARTY!!

Do you like parties? Think of social media as one big party. People are talking, laughing, and patting each other on the back. Some are gossiping in the corner. Friends are showing each other pictures of their pets and raving about the movies they saw last month. They're asking each other for advice about the best businesses in town.

What's the best part of this party? **Everyone's invited — including you!**

If you are not actively using social media, you're missing out - not just on a fun party, but also on loads of potential customers and income.

Since nearly two-thirds of Americans use social media, it's safe to say many of your customers are hanging out there. And even if you're not there yet, chances are they're already talking about you on social — nicely or not. So grab your dancing shows, and go join the social media party.

It's the perfect place to **promote your product, connect with customers, and reach new audiences.**

# *Nearly Two-Thirds Of Americans Use Social Media!*

# CHAPTER 12

# FOUR KEYS TO GOING FROM CONTENT TO CASH!

Can social media really help me sell more, or is this just theory? How can I get more people to engage me? How can social media help me to sell more? In this chapter I will show you how to go from content to cash! First, I asked some successful sales people (top income earners) to give me some examples of how social media could influence business and here are some of their thoughts:

- *I feel that social media is critical to sales on a retail level. · I have been using it for years. Messaging is the key.*

- *I have had great success with marketing myself on social media. One of the best ways is to stay consistent with the message, keep it genuine and super fun.*

- *I have had success using Facebook ads and placing personal posts via Facebook and connecting with new customers.*

- *I have had huge success, I just use bribes.*

- *The greatest use I've received from social media is to remind my friends and family an inner circle of what I do. Secondly I keep my profile public so I can be perceived as a real human being to prospective clients. finally I think I've created more deals buy online reviews than just social media presence.*

- *I post items on my down time (obviously, there's down time). I've joined a new group and would say that I've made 11 recent sales from posting. However, I've met a lot of people as a result of posting. Friends that I didn't have prior to.*

## 4 KEYS TO GOING FROM CONTENT TO CASH

## 1. PROMOTE YOUR PRODUCT

Product marketing is at the core of any effective digital marketing strategy. By distributing your product across various social media platforms, you'll make sure it's seen — and by the right people. Not only will you increase your credibility with current customers, you'll also attract new audiences that are likely to connect with your content and product resulting in more income. You are now moving from content to cash!

Use the **two/two/two rule**: post each piece twice within the first day of publishing, twice within the first week, and twice within the first month. Each post is handcrafted to deliver a new message each time. Incorporate it into your social strategy.

## 2. STAY CONNECTED WITH CUSTOMERS

A customer isn't done with your business just because they've completed the sales cycle. Once someone buys from you, your relationship is often just beginning. It's important to keep customers happy for a couple of reasons. First, you want them to speak highly of you to others so that you can acquire new customers and establish your reputation as the best salesperson around. Second, you want them to keep you in mind as their first choice for the next time they're looking to buy.

*re we share, the more we have..."*

So how do you maintain a relationship with your customers today? Joe Girard, The World's Greatest Salesman did it by the mail and the phone. You do it today by engaging with them on social media.

## 3. UNDERSTAND HUMAN NATURE

People like to brag about their purchases — especially big ones like homes, property or vehicles. It's just human nature. The reverse is also true: if a customer had a bad experience at your store (which we know would *never* happen), consequently they may want to rant about it on social media. **Negative messages will negatively impact your sales.**

## 4. REACH NEW AUDIENCES

Parties are a place for meeting new people - not crowding in a corner with your core group of friends.

The same is true with social media. If all you're doing is sharing your content with the same people every time, you're not putting yourself out there. Increase your exposure and generate new leads by reaching out to people who have never interacted with your brand before.

One simple yet powerful way to do this is the use of hash tags!

# Chapter 13

# HOW TO GET GOOD ONLINE REVIEWS

What motivates shoppers to write 5-star reviews?

This should be no surprise to anyone. Shoppers today are a savvy bunch. Before they step into a retail store, the consumer is likely to have done their homework; researching what best fits their needs and where to shop. They ask family, friends and co-workers what they like about their grocery store and where why the shop there. Another resource that has gained influence with consumers is online reviews. To some extent, businesses lack control over the information that influences consumers; however, you CAN endeavor to ensure that your online reviews reflect an overall positive experience that invites consumers to give you a shot at earning their business.

## TRUE OR FALSE

The majority of online reviews are submitted by disgruntled consumers with unreasonable expectations. We can attest that this statement is false! The Edmunds.com Reviews Team analyzed a one-month period of dealership reviews posted on Edmunds.com, and found that over 90% of the reviews published were positive reviews for either the sales or service department, and the most common title for **any** review was "Great Experience."

Here are some of the findings from our analysis to illuminate what qualities and experiences motivate consumers to write a 5-star review about a business.

Many consumers begin by stating that they did not anticipate enjoying the shopping or purchasing process, or were even dreading it, but go on to use these keywords and phrases repeatedly to describe their experience:

- No-pressure, didn't feel rushed
- Trustworthy
- They listened to me
- Quick and painless — made the process easy
- Quick and clear communication (email or in-person)
- No games
- Final price was exactly as negotiated (no last-minute surprises)
- Professional and polite salesperson
- Attentive to customer's needs
- Salesperson went above and beyond — locating a specific vehicle, delivering vehicle to customer, staying after hours, etc. Source: Edmunds.com

# CHAPTER 14

# WAYS TO WIN WITH YELP!

Getting great Yelp reviews is well worth the effort. I have been in businesses where salespeople are bored stiff, waiting for customers, while fully 50% of the Yelp reviews were terrible. Hello!!! Poor Yelp reviews drive traffic away from your business. My wife spends a lot of money and she never buys *anything* without reading the reviews. Most savvy customers (with good credit) read reviews first, before calling or visiting your dealership. The results of a study by Michael Luca, a professor at Harvard Business School, found that a one-star increase in a Yelp rating led to a corresponding 5-9 percent jump in revenue.

### *Several Ways to Get Reviews*

1. **Give customers a 'heads-up.'** Instead of saying "Write a review about our business on Yelp," say, "Check us out on Yelp, while you are waiting for the business manager." This is a "heads up" — an FYI that raises awareness.

2. **Put a 'Find us on Yelp' sign on or near the checkout counter.** You can make your own using Yelps brand assets or online jpegs.

3. **Add a link to your email signature.** Companies often overlook the marketing value of an email signature, but it's a subtle way to encourage Yelp reviews. Include the words mentioned in the first point: "Check us out on Yelp."

*re we share, the more we have..."*

4. **Share reviews on Facebook and Twitter.** You can have a positive impact as you share Yelp reviews on social networks like Facebook and Twitter.

5. **Use reviews in marketing materials.**

   - Don't take it out of context
   - Stay faithful to the reviewer

**DIGITAL WOM**

A review is another form of good old WOM (digital word of mouth). Reviews may not make or break you and your business, but the fact that people rely on others like themselves for recommendations when making purchase decisions is sufficient reason to take advantage of the marketing benefits they have to offer.

# THINKTANK

**THINK TANK**

WRITE ON SHORT PARAGRAPH ON WHY ONLINE REVIEWS ARE SO IMPORTANT TO YOU SALES SUCCESS:

_____

_____

_____

_____

_____

_____

_____

# CONCLUSION

The entire Social Media idea is all about influencing customers on the path to a sale. You have the power of influence in your digital strategy. One of the reasons social media is so interesting to me, is it allows people to create a following, generate massive exposure and make a lot of money by selling products without even having their own website!

What kind of results can you expect using social media?

- Social media can influence the sale of your product.
- It can help you create a community of raving fans.
- It can help you grow a list of potential buyers through referrals.
- It can help you build a solid reputation through reviews.

- Oh, did I mention that there's literally an endless supply of customers because it's the Internet and you can reach anyone, anywhere, at anytime?

Social Media is your channel to sales success today! Now let's look at a day-by-day strategy for a social media explosion!

# SOCIAL EXPLOSION ACTION STRATEGY

**MONDAY -** DO 3 YOUTUBE VIDEOS OF VARIOUS PRODUCTS

**TUESDAY -** SHARE 8-10 TWEETS – USE THE PROCESS

**WEDNESDAY OR THURSDAY**

POST THREE HOT PRODUCTS ON INSTAGRAM

POST VALUABLE BUSINESS INFORMATION ON LINKEDIN

**FRIDAY**

POST 8-10 ON FACEBOOK – RELEVANT, RECENT, LOCAL

**SATURDAY MORNING**

CHECK ALL SOCIAL MEDIA AND RESPOND WITH CTA

**ON EVERY SALE:**

POST ON FACEBOOK #RAVINGFAN

TAG THE GUEST

ASK FOR YELP REVIEWS

*re we share, the more we have..."*

## BERNARD SMALLS
### About Bernard Smalls

Bernard Smalls has functioned as a corporate trainer in the business world and as a consulting resource with a focus on leadership, sales, and service excellence for over 25 years. In a previous career, he was a professional drummer playing in the Oakland-San Francisco Bay Area.

After a potentially lucrative deal with Motown fell through, he began to pursue spiritual development. Bernard holds a Bachelor's Degree in Esoteric Theology and is the founder HuMax Consulting Group. Bernard brings timeless solutions to organizations through proven wisdom that produces the best results.

## SEMINARS & WORKSHOPS
## SOCIAL MEDIA SECRETS FOR CAR SALES

The world in general has grossly underestimated the power of social media. It's time for dealerships and car salespeople to awake to the power of social media. Bernard trains salespeople in simple rules for using Facebook, Twitter, Instagram, LinkedIn and YouTube.

## SALES EXCELLENCE

Most sales people see selling as a fight for the checkbook with the customer where the salesperson and customer are in an antagonistic relationship. This seminar holds key concepts of how to do it right and prosper in the world of professional selling.

## CUSTOMER SERVICE EXCELLENCE

Most people have not understood the direct connection between the quality of customer service and economics. Customer Service Excellence is a customer service workshop that will rev-up your

commitment and WOW your customers. Internationally acclaimed business experts Dr. Ken Blanchard, Dottie Walters and Peter J. Daniels have all personally endorsed Bernard's flagship book on Customer Service.

## LEADERSHIP EXCELLENCE

This workshop deals with concepts of organizational development, situational leadership and motivating your staff to high achievement.

## BERNARD SMALLS

P.O. BOX 724, SUWANEE, GEORGIA 30024 Phone: (678) 382-1556
www.socialmediasecretsforcarsales.com
www.humaxltd.com

www.ingramcontent.com/pod-product-compliance
Lightning Source LLC
Chambersburg PA
CBHW060011210526
45170CB00017B/2307